SSF

W9-BNU-645

S.S.F. Public Library
West Orange
840 West Orange Ave.
South San Francisco, CA 94080

FEB   2009

GAYLORD

Space Launch!

Let's Explore
Mercury

Helen and David Orme

GARETH**STEVENS**

GS

PUBLISHING

A Member of the WRC Media Family of Companies

Please visit our web site at: www.garethstevens.com
For a free color catalog describing Gareth Stevens Publishing's
list of high-quality books and multimedia programs, call
1-800-542-2595 (USA) or 1-800-387-3178 (Canada).
Gareth Stevens Publishing's fax: (414) 332-3567.

Library of Congress Cataloging-in-Publication Data

Orme, Helen.
    Let's explore Mercury / Helen and David Orme.
        p. cm. — (Space launch!)
    Includes index.
    ISBN-13: 978-0-8368-7942-1 (lib. bdg.)
    ISBN-13: 978-0-8368-8127-1 (softcover)
    1. Mercury (Planet)—Juvenile literature. 2. Mercury (Planet)—Exploration—
Juvenile literature. I. Orme, David, 1948 Mar. 1- II. Title.
QB611.O76   2007
523.41—dc22   2006034714

This North American edition first published in 2007 by
Gareth Stevens Publishing
A Member of the WRC Media Family of Companies
330 West Olive Street, Suite 100
Milwaukee, Wisconsin 53212 USA

This U.S. edition copyright © 2007 by Gareth Stevens, Inc. Original edition copyright © 2006 by ticktock Entertainment
Ltd. First published in Great Britain in 2006 by ticktock Media Ltd., Unit 2, Orchard Business Centre, North Farm Road,
Tunbridge Wells, Kent, TN2 3XF, United Kingdom.

The publishers would like to thank: Sandra Voss, Tim Bones, James Powell, Indexing Specialists (UK) Ltd.

Ticktock project editor: Julia Adams
Ticktock project designer: Emma Randall

Gareth Stevens Editorial Direction: Mark Sachner
Gareth Stevens Editors: Barbara Kiely Miller and Carol Ryback
Gareth Stevens Art Direction: Tammy West
Gareth Stevens Designer: Dave Kowalski

Photo credits (t=top, b=bottom, c=center, l=left, r=right, bg=background)
ESA: 23bl; Hemera: 15tl; NASA: front cover, 1, 6br, 8cr, 11br, 18b, 19tr, 19bl, 21tl, 22cr, 23tr; Science Photo Library: 4–5bg (original), 9tl, 9bl,
10bl, 11tl; Shutterstock: 3bg, 6bl, 8cl, 9ctl, 9cbl, 13tr, 13bl; ticktock picture archive: 5tr, 6–7bg, 7tl, 7br, 9cr, 10–11bg, 11c, 12bl, 12br, 14bl, 14tr,
14–15bg, 15br, 16tr, 16bl, 17tr, 17bl, 18–19bg, 20tr, 20cr, 20bl, 20br, 21br, 22–23bg. Rocket drawing Dave Kowalski/© Gareth Stevens, Inc.

Every effort has been made to trace the copyright holders for the photos used in this book. The publisher apologizes,
in advance, for any unintentional omissions and would be pleased to insert the appropriate acknowledgements in
any subsequent edition of this publication.

All rights reserved. No part of this book may be reproduced, stored in a retrieval system, or transmitted
in any form or by any means, electronic, mechanical, photocopying, recording, or otherwise, without the
prior written permission of the publisher.

Printed in Canada

1 2 3 4 5 6 7 8 9 10 10 09 08 07 06

Contents

Where Is Mercury?

There are eight known planets in our **solar system**. The planets travel around the Sun. Mercury is the closest planet to the Sun.

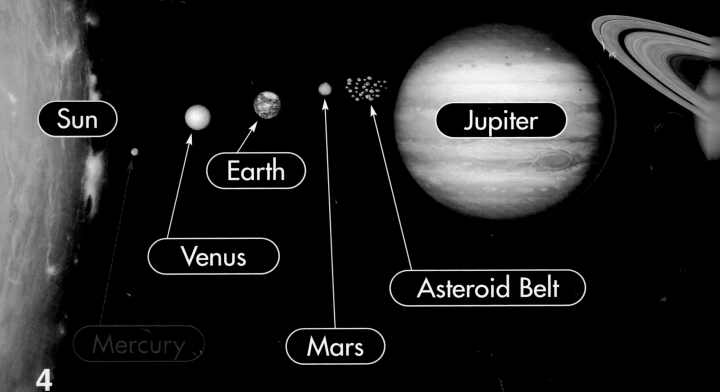

Sun

Earth

Venus

Jupiter

Asteroid Belt

Mercury

Mars

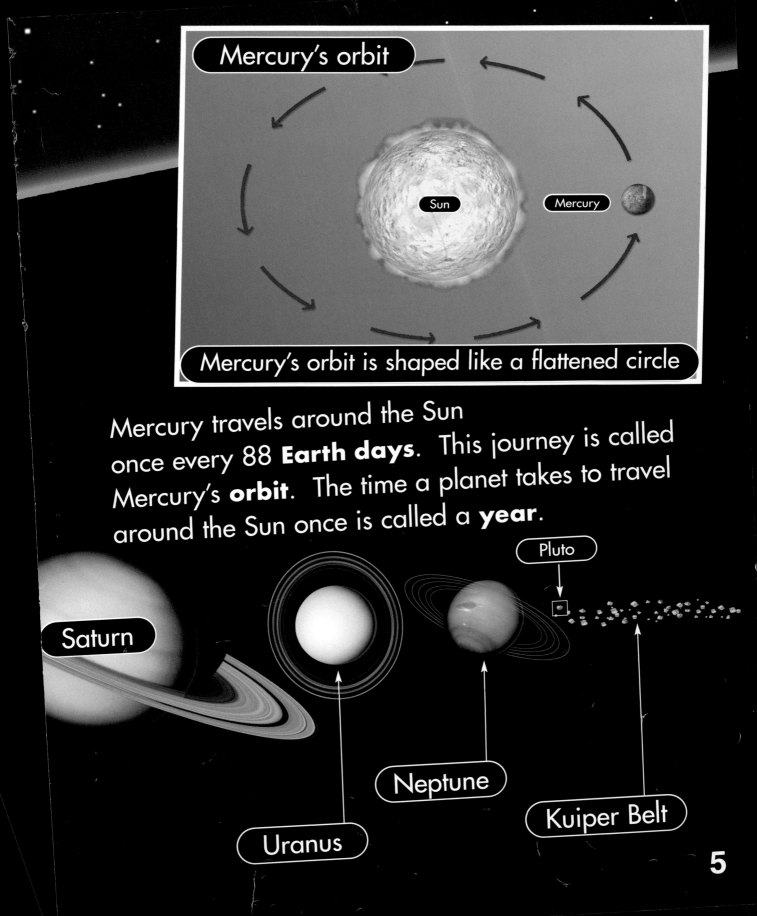

Mercury's orbit

Sun

Mercury

Mercury's orbit is shaped like a flattened circle

Mercury travels around the Sun once every 88 **Earth days**. This journey is called Mercury's **orbit**. The time a planet takes to travel around the Sun once is called a **year**.

Pluto

Saturn

Neptune

Uranus

Kuiper Belt

Planet Facts

Mercury is a small, rocky planet. It is the smallest planet in our solar system. Mercury orbits the Sun faster than any other planet. It travels 30 miles (48 kilometers) per second!

7,926 miles
(12,753 kilometers)

3,032 miles
(4,875 km)

Earth

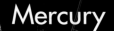

Mercury

core

inside Mercury

Mercury is a very heavy planet. Scientists think this is because the core, or center, of the planet is made of **iron**. The iron core is very thick and heavy.

A planet is always spinning around. The time a planet takes to spin around once is called a day. One day on Mercury is the same length of time as 59 Earth days!

direction of spin

What's the Weather Like?

Mercury is the closest planet to the Sun. Mercury's location is the reason why it is one of the hottest planets.

IMAGINE...
During the day, it is hot enough on Mercury to melt **lead**!

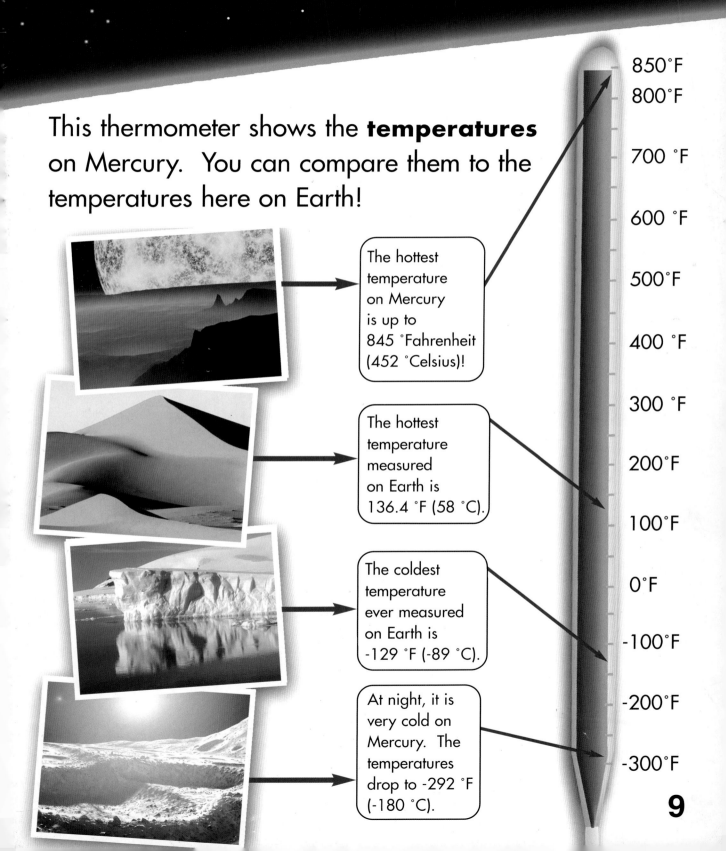

This thermometer shows the **temperatures** on Mercury. You can compare them to the temperatures here on Earth!

The hottest temperature on Mercury is up to 845 °Fahrenheit (452 °Celsius)!

The hottest temperature measured on Earth is 136.4 °F (58 °C).

The coldest temperature ever measured on Earth is -129 °F (-89 °C).

At night, it is very cold on Mercury. The temperatures drop to -292 °F (-180 °C).

850°F
800°F
700 °F
600 °F
500°F
400 °F
300 °F
200°F
100°F
0°F
-100°F
-200°F
-300°F

9

On the Surface

The surface of Mercury has huge cliffs and cracks. They are hundreds of miles long and up to 1.9 miles (3 km) high! The cliffs were probably made millions of years ago.

1.9 miles
(3 km)

Mercury was very, very hot when it was a new planet. The huge cracks formed across its surface when Mercury cooled down.

Mercury also has one of the largest **craters** in the solar system. It measures about 839 miles (1,350 km) across!

This crater, called the Caloris Basin, was created when a huge rock hit the surface of Mercury. Vibrations went right through the planet and cracked the surface on the other side!

This is a photograph of half of the Caloris Basin.

Ice on Mercury

In 1991, scientists thought they found ice at Mercury's North Pole. This discovery is very important because ice is frozen water. Life is only possible with water, so scientists always look for water on planets.

Mercury's North Pole

This is the Arecibo **radio telescope** in Puerto Rico. Scientists used it to look for ice on Mercury. It is one of the largest telescopes in the world.

At Mercury's North Pole, there are places where the Sun's heat never reaches, so the ice there would never melt. These places may be in the shadow of cliffs or at the bottom of craters.

crater

comet

The ice may have come from deep inside Mercury. It may also have come from **comets** that crashed into its surface.

13

Finding Mercury

For thousands of years, people have studied the sky. In the beginning, they didn't even have telescopes.

We can see Mercury without a telescope in the morning...

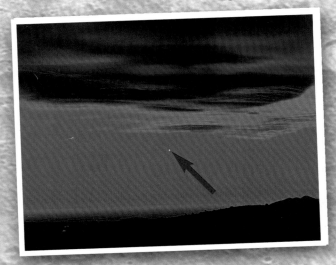

...and the evening.

People in ancient Greece knew Mercury was one planet, but they still gave it two names. They called it Apollo in the morning and Hermes in the evening.

Mercury

Ancient Romans gave the planet the name Mercury. They named the fast-moving planet after their god of travel, who was also the messenger of the gods.

This telescope was invented by English scientist Isaac Newton in 1668. Scientists using the telescope were able to see and study Mercury much more easily.

What Can We See?

You can see Mercury in the early morning and as it gets dark at night.

For the best view of Mercury, you should use a small telescope after the Sun has set.

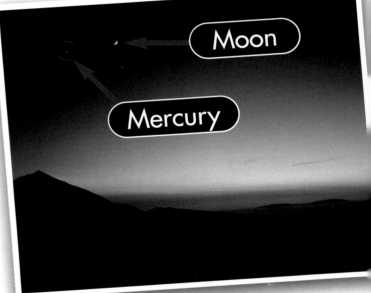

Moon

Mercury

Mercury is easier to see if you live in the southern half of the world.

Mercury is difficult to see from Earth. We have to look toward the Sun to see Mercury, which is very tiny compared to the Sun. Looking at the Sun is also very dangerous.

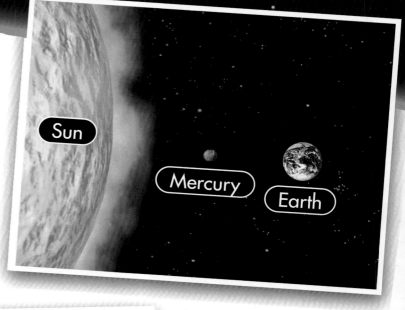

Astronomers study Mercury when it moves in front of the Sun, using special telescopes. This happens only about 13 times every 100 years.

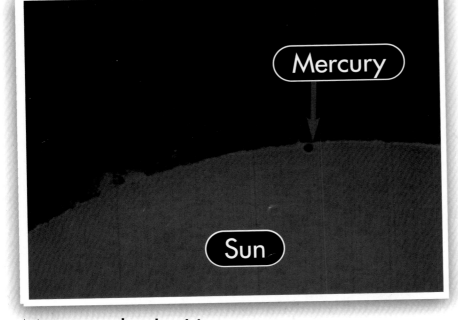

Mercury looks like a tiny black dot against the Sun.   17

Missions to Mercury

Sending a **space probe** to Mercury is difficult because it is so close to the Sun. Unless scientists are very careful, the spacecraft would be burned up by the Sun!

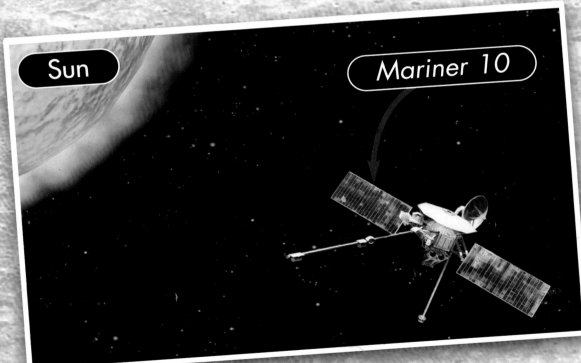

Sun

Mariner 10

Mariner 10 is the only space probe to have reached Mercury. It arrived there in 1974 and flew closely by the planet three times.

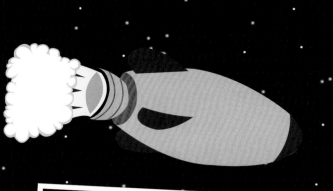

During its three fly-bys, *Mariner 10* was able to photograph almost half of Mercury's surface. It also sent back information about the temperatures on the planet.

28 miles
(45 km)

Mariner 10 took pictures showing more detail of the surface, too. This photo is of a huge crater on Mercury. It is called the Degas Crater. It is 28 miles (45 km) wide! **19**

Mercury Discoveries

Space probes are not the only way we can find out about planets. We can use telescopes based right here on Earth.

Some telescopes let us see farther than others. The small photos on this page show how well Mercury can be seen from different kinds of telescopes.

home telescope

scientist's telescope

This is a picture of Mercury taken by a radio telescope.

Mercury's North Pole

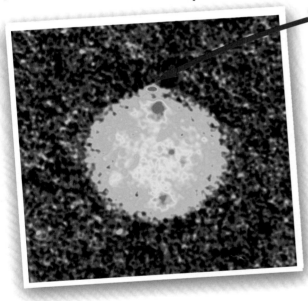

The different colors tell scientists about the temperatures of the planet's surface. The top red area is the North Pole, where scientists think they have found ice.

radio telescope

Future Explorations

MESSENGER (short for **ME**rcury **S**urface, **S**pace **EN**vironment, **GE**ochemistry and **R**anging mission) was launched by **NASA** in August 2004. It is the second mission to Mercury.

MESSENGER should fly past Mercury in 2008 and 2009. It will go into orbit around the planet in 2011.

MESSENGER will photograph the surface of the whole planet. It will send back much more information about its **atmosphere** and what Mercury is made of.

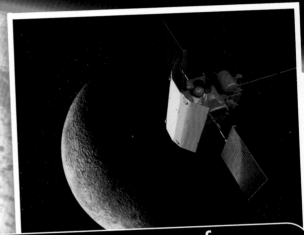

a painting of **MESSENGER** near Mercury

a painting of Bepi-Colombo near Mercury

European and Japanese scientists have planned a mission to Mercury for 2013. It will be called *Bepi-Colombo*. Its two spacecraft should reach Mercury in 2019. They will help make a very exact map of Mercury. **23**

Glossary

asteroid a rocky object that orbits the Sun. Most asteroids orbit the Sun between Mars and Jupiter.

atmosphere the gases that surround a planet, moon, or star

astronomers people who study outer space, often using telescopes

comets objects usually made of ice and frozen dirt and gas that are in orbit around the Sun

craters holes in the surface of a planet or moon made either by a volcano or when the planet or moon is hit by a rock from space

Earth day a day is the time it takes a planet to spin around once. A day on Earth is 24 hours long.

iron a very hard and strong metal

lead a heavy gray metal. It melts at about 620 °F (327 °C)

NASA (short for National Aeronautics and Space Administration) a group of scientists and astronauts who research space

orbit the path that a planet or other object takes when traveling around the Sun, or the path a satellite takes around a planet

radio telescope a tool to help find out about a planet that is very far away. A radio telescope uses special signals called radio waves to learn about the temperatures and the surface of a planet.

solar system the Sun and everything that is in orbit around it

space probe spacecraft sent from Earth to explore the solar system

temperatures how hot or cold things are

year the time it takes a planet to make a single orbit around the Sun

Index